Creating Peace Through Grieving Process

DAXSON PUBLISHING

On Death

I

    Can death be sleep, when life is but a dream,
    And scenes of bliss pass as a phantom by?
    The transient pleasures as a vision seem,
    And yet we think the greatest pain's to die.

II

    How strange it is that man on earth should roam,
    And lead a life of woe, but not forsake
    His rugged path; nor dare he view alone
    His future doom which is but to awake.

By: John Keats

Creating Peace Through Grieving Process

Foreword by: Cindy Doss
By Erica B. Castro

Creating Peace Through the Grieving Process
© 2024, Erica B. Castro
ISBN:979-8-9900531-4-4
Library of Congress Control Number: 2024912140

Cover Photo by: Leonard Carrillo
Graphic art by: Lola Rose Fernandez

First Edition, 2024

Printed in the United States of America

Edited by: Maria d. Duarte Ortiz
Cover Design by Rachel Kiskaddon
Layout Design by Rachel Kiskaddon

Published by: Daxson Publishing Los Angeles, Ca, 90022

Dedication

This book is for my mother Maria R. Castro who unknowingly
would inadvertently teach me about death.

My mother and Me

Foreword

I highly recommend Erica B. Castro's book *Creating Peace Through the Grieving Process* to all who have suffered the loss of a loved one. Losing a loved one can be devastating, but after reading this book you will realize that although our loved ones have crossed over, they continue to exist in the spirit world. They can send us signs to let us know they are still with us. In the book Erica guides us through the practices that will help us communicate with our loved ones in spirit.

There are many things I love about this book. I very much appreciate how Erica bares her soul and bravely shares her personal journey as she looks back on how dealing with grief and loss has impacted her life. In sharing the wisdom and knowledge she has gained from these experiences she offers insight on how to navigate the onslaught of emotions that can overwhelm us in our bereavement and she lets us know that we are not alone. We can take comfort knowing our loved ones are near.

The book is filled with personal accounts of people that have received signs from their loved ones in the spirit world. These accounts also include those who have had some type of communication with their loved ones that have passed.

This book is a must-read for all who seek the comfort and peace that comes from staying connected to our loved ones in the spirit world.

By: Cindy Doss
Psychic/ Medium

Table of Contents

Acknowledgments

I am beyond grateful for all your love and support. I want to thank my brother Javier, and my sister Jessica who believed in me when I could not believe in myself. I want to thank my brother Tony for having to raise me because my dad had to work. I want to thank my soul sister Dr. Melba Stetz who has pushed me to be a better version of myself *"te amo hermana."* To my psychic friends Kristi Thompson and Jessica Nichole thank you so much for your support and love. To my mentor Alyson Gannon, thank you for your belief in me. I do not know where I would be without you guys. To my coach, Regeline Gigi Sabbat from Life Service Centers of America, thank you for all your global virtual panels and for advocating for those without a voice. To my long time coach, Navi Bliss, without your guidance there is no way this would be possible. Thank you for dragging me out of my comfort zone. To my friend Yvette Figueroa thank you for being there when I was lost. To my friend Kay Lambert, you have given me hope when I had none thank you. Cindy Doss thank your for always supporting me. To my family, Leonard Carrillo, thank you for all the work you had to do when I was writing, taking classes, speaking, and being there for our kids when I could not. I really appreciate you helping me make this possible. Little Leonard, Rhiannon, Melody, Daniel, thank you for being patient with me and supporting me, I love you guys so much. Lupita, and Mikey than you so much for being you both have filled my life with joy, and I am proud to be your aunt. To my niece Isabel, I love you. Dante, Daisy, my princess Azalea, Easton, and Daxson thank you so much for all your support and always being there when I have needed you. To my work sisters, in the Schurr high school English department there is no way I would be able to survive teaching high school without you guys thank you for your unconditional acceptance. To my students, past and present you have impacted my life in so many ways. I am so grateful our lives crossed because in the year we shared as teacher and student I took a little piece of each of you and it made me a better person thank you.

Preface

I wrote this book because many of my relatives have transitioned across the rainbow, and during the grieving process I struggled tremendously. I wish there was a guide or a way for me to realize that my loved ones were always with me. I lost my mom at five years old, and I wish I could call out to her, and know that she was there with me. In my journey, I have discovered that grief can be overwhelming, and extremely painful. I wrote this book so you can possibly practice these suggestions to feel your loved ones nearby. This book does not take you through the seven stages of grief, but it gives you exercises and hope to connect with your loved ones, and for you to know they are always with you. I am so sorry for your loss, but just know that one day you will be with your loved ones again when you meet them in the spirit world. Sending you so much love and prayers.

Things I Remember About My Mother

I have few memories of my mother
She died and left me, I was only five
I remember her cooking

That roasted chicken smell
Rosemary, thyme, basil, spices
The white rice
And fresh salad
I remember pistachio pudding

I remember her washing dishes
Cutting her hand
Getting stitches

Her throwing up
Yellow bile
Her losing her hair

I remember mother's day
The cake my dad got her

Or the soft boiled eggs
She cooked me
She would call me by my middle name
Betty

I remember her praying
At night
Waiting for my dad
I remember her crying

I remember her orange outfit
The pattern of her funeral
a purple sequinced suit

I remember our last goodbye
My final kiss
I was first

My sister was second
She died and left us behind

I miss her embrace
Her warm touch
Looking at her face

She loved me
Although memories
Are fragmented
She has been with me

I have no proof
I just know her love
Transcended in death

And somehow she was always there

I Know What It's Like

I am so sorry for your loss, and I know what it is like to lose loved ones and wake up and wonder how I was going to make it through the day, or how I was going to get myself out of bed. I learned about loss at a very young age. My mother died when I was five years old, and it was very traumatic for my young five-year-old mind. From the moment she died, and I saw her in her coffin I had this overpowering fear that I was next and that I was going to die. My overactive imagination came up with different scenarios of how I could die. I lived engulfed in fear of death at a very young age, and I lived with all the what ifs. What if my mother had lived, how would my life be different? I carried this empty space of longing and yearning for a mother, and I always felt left out because I did not have one. I am a strong believer today though that if you focus on what you do not have, you will miss out on the things you do have. I was sad, lost and constantly looking for external forces to fill the emptiness I carried. What I have realized is that I have accomplished so many things without my mother that I have forgotten what life was like with her. I wanted her, I wish I had her, but I had overcome so many challenges, that I have thrived without her. Losing those people you love can create an empty space and can make you feel like you are all alone, but it does not have to be that way.

I did not realize that we can connect with our loved ones on so many different levels, and that our loved ones never leave us. They are always with us, and there are things that we can practice on a daily basis to connect to those we love because no matter what they live around us in the spiritual world. They never leave us, but we have to learn to put our thoughts aside and pay attention to the signs and the messages they give us from the other side. In so many ways, our loved ones want to communicate and love being with us, but our own minds get in the way of the message. We discount their communication, as something else, or as something our brain made up. We need to have trust and have faith that our loved ones love us so much, they miss us as well, and they want to say, "I love you," and "I am here." We just have to be open and be aware of their essence to receive their messages.

There have been two specific times that I felt the presence of my mother. In my twenties I was purely logical, so I often discounted messages that could have been for me from my loved ones who passed. I was not connected to the spiritual realm. Even though I had several spiritual encounters, I did not really believe the messages from spirits that were sent to me. You must create or start a spiritual practice. What I mean by this, a practice where you connect to the spiritual realm, and in this practice, you will create trust, so you can believe and receive the messages sent to you from loved ones. What I mean by the spiritual realm is like a dream state, where everything feels real. It is like dreaming with people who have passed, and you feel them, can talk to them, and it feels so real. You can do that through deep meditation as well and connect to your loved ones.

The first time my mother came to me was when I was in labor with my son. I was twenty-two years old, and my ex-husband was working nights at the time. I was having strong contractions five minutes apart, but I was only one centimeter. I was alone, and scared as I was experiencing labor alone. I was afraid because I was going through so much pain, and with no one by my side. I had no idea what was happening to my body. I was in labor, and I didn't know how to deal or cope with it. Then all of a sudden, I felt my mother's presence and she was not alone. I felt both my mother and my grandmother's presence. My grandmother was the woman people went to so she could heal them, she was what is known as a medicine woman. She once helped a child correct his stutter in an orthodox way. She put a cicada in that child's mouth, and the child never stuttered again. I knew why my grandmother was there. She was watching over my labor, and my mother was there for support. I was finally able to enter a relaxed state and feel safe. I was able to get some rest because I knew that I was not alone, I had the essence of these two spirits loving and protecting me, and my fear dissipated. I knew they were there. I could feel them around me, and I had no doubt. Possibly, I was able to accept their presence because I was in labor and I was desperate, and that put my mind in check, but I had no doubt that I was physically alone in that room, but spiritually I was surrounded.

The second time I felt them both again was when I was in labor with my second child. This time it was different. With my first birth, I endured the pain without medication. The contractions were five minutes apart, and I had a minute to rest. With the birth of my daughter the contractions were thirty seconds apart, and I could not handle the pain, so I was on medication. I was nervous because during my labor my whole body was shaking, and I could not control my shivers. I was not cold. It was my body's response to the pain. At that moment, I felt calm, and I felt my mother and my grandmother again. Their essence and love were present, and I knew that my baby and I were going to be alright. I just knew that being with them nothing bad could possibly happen. I felt their strength, their faith, and confidence that my labor was going to be successful with no complications. I believe our loved ones want us to know of their presence. To reassure us that we are going to be okay, and that we are loved. They are with us no matter what.

There are so many things you can do to connect with your loved ones. There are exercises you can do to be connected to them. They are never gone, and when you feel that feeling in your gut that they are near, it's because they are. You can feel their energy, their essence, sometimes you can smell them, at other times they can communicate through electronic devices. Our loved ones are always there watching us go through our processes, and our life. They are our cheerleaders on the other side who want to guide us, love us, and be there for us.

I know that grief is hard. I completely understand. I have been there several times. I know you miss your loved ones' presence or conversations, but you can work hard to connect with them. You can speak to them out loud, you can write them letters, you can listen to music and visualize the smile on their faces. These are just some things you can do to connect to your loved ones and feel their love.

The truth is, grief is going to happen, and by now you are probably aware that grief happens in waves. What I can say is that our loved ones do not want to see us sad and depressed. Of course, you have to go through the grieving process, but you have to do the emotional work to lift yourself out of it. With that, know that you are not alone and that you can get through this process I promise you.

I lost my dad at the age of 27. Two weeks later I lost a cousin who was only 33 years old to a sudden heart attack. I loved them both dearly. When my father died, I was in a very toxic marriage, and although we tried to work things out and go to counseling, we could not break our dysfunctional patterns. I was dealing with the loss of my father, my cousin, and the sadness I carried daily because I did not feel supported by my ex-husband, but worst of all I had no self-love, and I could not support myself emotionally. I was going to therapy, and when my therapist saw my emotional state, she told me I needed to admit myself to a mental hospital. I was shocked, but at the same time, I trusted my therapist, and I went into the hospital. When I was in the hospital, I was surrounded by so many people with a lot more issues than mine. I had compassion for these people. I did not understand their mental illness, but I knew what it was like to be incredibly sad. I participated in every activity or group they offered. I felt like I did not belong, but at the same time, I tried to learn as much as I could while I was there.

At the same time, I was open to learning and growing. I was at that mental hospital for five days; they didn't want to release me on the final day because they needed more observation. In my fear of not being let out, I prayed to God that they would release me. I went in voluntarily, and I was on medication, but they wanted to make sure I was fine. I no longer wanted to be there, and my doctor did not want to release me. When I prayed, I felt my father, and the realization and message I got was that my father was going to be with me always. I lived in California, and he lived in Texas, and now for the rest of my life I could connect with my father because he was going to be with me always. Once I felt that calmness and confidence that my father was there and the feeling that he was never going to leave me, I felt assured that they would release me from the hospital. They had me sign up for a bereavement group, and after that they released me. Our loved ones are always with us, and they sometimes help us in our earthly situations like my father gave me the calmness I needed for the hospital to release me.

Losing our loved ones is difficult, but I believe they are in a better place. I believe their soul and essence continues, and although it hurts you can gain the strength and confidence to overcome it. They do not want us to be sad, they want us to follow our dreams and create the life we want. They want us to find peace in living, to experience joy, and not take things for granted. They want us to experience life and enjoy every moment; our loved ones want us to be grateful for the beautiful moments in life. They want us to do all the things we have always wanted to do, and they want us to overcome our fears. There is no fear on the other side, so they want us to be fearless and do all those things we are afraid to do. In other words, consider what you would do, try, or learn if you were guaranteed success? They want us to live and learn from mistakes and use failure as steppingstones towards greatness. They want you to learn from their mistakes and be better because they loved and taught you. Their hope for you is to love without reservations. They want us to live without holding back. They want us to have faith without any doubts. Our loved ones want us to have all the beauty of life and enjoy every moment, good or bad, because there's always a greater purpose for every single moment in life.

When going through grief, you must honor yourself and your feelings. You must lean into your feelings. Most of us are never taught how to feel feelings. Most of us want to eat them away, keep busy, shop, or use substances to numb feelings. When going through grief embrace your feelings and thank them. I know this is difficult, and it is hard to accept the loss, but the best thing you can do with feelings is to experience them. The more you try to avoid your feelings the harder and more difficult it can become. Feelings are what make us human, and that is why it is so important to feel through those feelings. To be your true authentic self, you have to honor and love your feelings. Feelings can be uncomfortable, but you must embrace all the difficult parts of you. Losing a loved one brings up feelings that you are not used to, but those feelings are meant to be lived and experienced. The best thing you can do in your grieving process is to love your feelings and be grateful that you had the opportunity to love.

I Wish I Could have...

It is never too late to create those memories you wish you had with your loved ones, you can call their spirits in. In many instances when a person dies, we are still living and carrying regret. Sometimes people die unexpectedly, and when that happens, we hoped we had made time for that person, but we never did because life was too busy. We cannot go back in time and change this, but our loved ones do not want us to hold on to regret. They want us to be happy, and live life to the fullest. One of the best things I have discovered a person can do is to do what you wanted to do with them and call their spirit in. It is never too late to create a memory with someone who passed. I know it sounds unorthodox, and you are probably doubting the possibility, but it is possible.

One of the things that was very difficult for me was losing my father. We lived far apart in life, and I always wanted him to see my son play baseball. The happiest moments of my life were when my son played baseball. I always wanted my father to be there with me as I watched my son hit the ball, run bases, or field the ball. I know my father loved my children greatly, so I know that watching my son would have made him happy. So, one day, I saw another grandfather at the park supporting his grandson, and I did feel a pang of jealousy. I questioned why my father was not here, and why he was not experiencing my son's game. Then suddenly, I realized my father was there and he had the best seat in the house because he had an aerial view of the field, and he could sit next to me or go in the field and be next to my son. So, I closed my eyes, meditated and cleared my mind. Then I pictured my father with a big smile excited to be at the game. I heard him cheering for my son, and I saw his unbelievable joy. I felt his essence and presence, and a breeze crossed my body. I imagined him holding my hand, and I felt his love. He was such an incredible grandfather, and above all he loved his grandkids. Although he was physically gone, his energy, and his spirit were there. I used my mind to talk to him because I did not want to look like a crazy woman, but I was so connected with my father at that moment.

Meditation is so important when connecting with our loved ones. This is because we must put our thoughts to rest and trust our spirit to find a way. It is our logical mind that separates us from their essence. When you practice meditation, you get your thoughts to slow down, and you try to let go of the thoughts that do interfere with your connection. When you have a clear mind, and you are deep in meditation, your awareness of your senses becomes unclouded. You can hear small sounds, you can visualize clearly, you can smell sharply, and your body feels every little sensation. When you get into the high meditative state, your senses then are heightened, and you are then able to feel your loved ones wrapping their energy around you.

My mentor, Alyson Gannon has put together a book from different mediums who expressed their direct experiences in their life connecting with their loved ones who passed. The book is called *The Last Breath* curated by: Alyson Gannon. Alyson´s mother died unexpectedly, and she felt bad that she had a negative attitude in putting her mother's make-up on. Her mother always loved it when Alyson did her make-up. After her unexpected passing Alyson was sad about her previous attitude. Suddenly, she realized that she could connect with her mother and do her mother's make-up even though her mother was in spirit. So, she created a sacred space, meditated and connected with her mother, and put on her make-up spiritually. She lived through a special moment even though her mother was gone. We can always connect with those we love.

We can sit on a park bench, meditate and in that moment connect with our loved ones and talk to them in our mind. We can tell them everything we want to say. We can tell them how much we love them and miss them. We can talk to them about our day or any major decisions we have coming up. We can talk to them about the kids. Their essence, and their spirit is real. The answers to our questions are those immediate thoughts that come to our minds. I know it seems like we answer our own questions, but we do not. These answers come from them as a way to communicate with us. Our loved ones are the same people, and how they would respond in real life is the same way they would respond in spirit. You are not having a conversation with yourself, the thoughts that come into your mind are what they would say, those thoughts are how they would respond. For these practices to work, you must trust and believe that the communication is coming from your loved ones. It is their essence and love that brings those answers to your mind.

Just recently I had a conversation with my father while I was sitting on a park bench. I closed my eyes, and I pictured him next to me with his arm around me holding my hand. My father was so loving. I told him I was worried about my siblings. He was grateful for my love and concern, but he said in Spanish, "*yo me encargo de ellos.*" What he said was "I will take care of them, and you focus on your life, do not worry I am with all of you." I understood that there was no use in worrying, and that he had a direct line to God because he was in heaven, and he would take care of it and ask God to help them.

Many of us do not realize that our loved ones have a direct line to God. They are in heaven. They are with the almighty, and they could pray to God or ask God for help. They can advocate on your behalf. Have faith in your loved ones. They are there for you, and they love you, and they want you to live the best possible life that you can.

Make a list of things that you miss doing with your loved one, or possibly make a list of things you miss them doing like baking bread, or watching a specific show, or praying. Once you have your list, you meditate and connect with your loved one, and you do those things with them. You can connect with grandma, make banana bread, and feel her presence, love, and guidance in the process of making bread. If you played a board game with your loved one, then you can roll the dice for both of you and listen to your thoughts as the game progresses because they are trying to speak to you. If you are winning, your loved one could be saying you always win, and yes, it is not your mind, it is them saying, you always win. If you went hiking with your loved one, connect, meditate, and take your loved one along for the walk. Again, the thoughts that come to your head are your loved one speaking to you.

My father loved certain shows and movies. I only remembered some, so I asked my siblings to remind me what shows he liked. The ones I personally remembered were *The Fugitive*, and any movie with Clint Eastwood. He loved action movies with Chuck Norris and Charles Bronson, as well as detective movies. In my childhood, I remembered him watching *Hill Street Blues*, and my sister reminded me that every Friday night, we would watch *Miami Vice*. My brother reminded me about the *Dirty Dozen*, and any movie with John Wayne in it. I decided then at that point to choose something to watch that my father would enjoy watching, and sit with him watching the show, feeling his presence next to me, and letting my thoughts be how he communicated with me. I just relished in the moment of what he enjoyed, and at the same time feeling his essence next to me.

There are so many things you can invite your loved ones to participate in. They can come to your outings or events. They are there already, but if you make a conscious intention, they will be there. You can feel them, and you can hear them through your thoughts as well.

If your loved ones always wanted to go to Ireland, for example, you can go and invite them with you. There are so many stories where people have gone to a place that their loved ones wanted to go to, and the person found a sign of their loved one there, or they had a moment where they felt the loved ones' essence. You can live out those dreams for your loved ones, if you are inclined to do so because it would make them happy. They want us to dare to live big, and to take risks because that is where we will learn the most. So many people live their life based on fear, and they never take risks or live the life they always dreamed of. Our loved ones passed, so they know what life for a spirit is like, so they know they want us to live the best life possible with no reservations.

Honor anniversaries, birthdays, fathers' days, or any special occasion for your loved ones who have passed. For the past five years, my daughter has bought a cake for my father on his birthday. We sing him happy birthday, as if he is there, and nothing makes my daughter so happy as to honor her grandfather on his birthday. Every time we go to visit Texas, we always go and visit the grave site where my parents are buried. For my daughter, it is a special moment because she adored her grandfather. My father died when my daughter was only four years old, but she remembers his love, and is grateful for all the memories he has left her. She honors him with every opportunity she has. You can honor the anniversary of when your loved one's died, their birthday, or any special day that connects you to them. This will connect you to them more, and it will bring them so much joy that you remember them, and you honor them.

Altars or *ofrendas* are very special to our loved ones. They appreciate that we keep them in our hearts and memory, and when we make an *ofrenda* or put their pictures up, we are honoring that their life mattered. We are saying I am so grateful you lived, and without you I would not be here, so thank you for your life and your existence. Having an altar or *ofrenda* for our loved ones is one of the best ways to honor them. Every time we see their pictures, they remind us of who they were and how much they loved us. If we hold on to the love they have for us, and relish in their essence, then we can get out of the grief stage and be grateful that they loved us.

Love is all around

Sometimes a person dies, and they have unresolved issues with the living. Which is often the case. For example, there are stories of people getting in an argument with a loved one, and then suddenly that person dies in a car accident. In other cases, maybe a person has left things unsaid, and then dies. Then they try to communicate with the living by showing signs of love such as: feathers, coins, butterflies, rainbows, and ladybugs.

I believe that spirits are at a higher form of consciousness, and fears or minor tribulations of this world do not matter to them. I feel like our loved ones are wrapped in unconditional love, and many of the things that mattered to them while living are obsolete.

One of the things I have done in my life is go to live mediumship readings to witness the medium connecting with their loved ones. There was a lady whose father passed away. She came to the show with her mother, and suddenly, a feisty mother-in-law came through, and the mother-in-law was asking the mother of the lady for forgiveness. She was saying that she was wrong, and that she really should not have treated her badly. She said that she knew she was a good person, and she was wrong. Then he started talking to the daughter about her dad, when suddenly, the grandmother on the father's side interjected and said, "well, does she forgive me or not?" The mother responded "yes." Sometimes the things that are important for us on earth do not matter on the other side.

After death it is almost like the ego lessens or even dies, and the things that are centered around love come forth because at the end of the day the most important aspect of a human being is love. Love dissipates so much negativity, and the people who have passed and loved us want us to have peace.

Guilt serves no purpose. If you have guilt, you need to process the guilt and release it. Understand that you cannot go back in time and change what has happened, but what you can do is make amends by changing the behavior you have guilt about. When we think of our loved ones, they do not want us to think of or carry guilt and feel bad about past discussions or past differences. They want us to be free emotionally, and to live the best life possible. However, if you are carrying guilt because you may not have done something, or said something, then there are ways to connect with our loved ones and release our guilt.

One common way to release our guilt is to write a letter to our loved one and go to their graveside or where their ashes were spread and read the letter out loud. Now if your loved one is laid to rest far away from you, then you can just go to a place in nature and read the letter out loud. Our loved ones are with us no matter how far apart we are geographically; in the world of spirits there are no constraints tied to time and space. Our loved ones see our heart and thoughts, and they want us to free ourselves from any guilt or anger that we may carry because those feelings only hold us down. You can always say sorry or ask for forgiveness and feel their love and their essence wrapped around your heart.

An example could be the following letter I wrote to my mother:

Dear Mother,

I want to say that I love you so very much. I wish I would have had you longer in my life, but I am so grateful that God chose you to be my mother. When you died, I experienced a sense of abandonment, and often for many periods of my life I felt alone. In my five-year-old mind, I blamed you for dying and leaving me to fend for my life on my own. I felt lost, unprotected, and alone without you. Whenever there were events and all my friends had their mothers there, I felt left out because you were gone. For twenty years, I felt like there was something wrong with me because I was carrying around this empty space without you. I failed to see that you were always with me, and

although you were gone your love transcended time and space. I had no idea that I could call you, and you would be there showing me love. Thank you so much for the times you wrapped me with your love. I am sorry for my anger and hurt, dear mother, just know I did not know any better. I love you so very much, and I am so grateful to know today that you never left me. Thank you for your love, and for watching over your grandkids. I am forever grateful for the five years I had you in this life and when my time is up, I cannot wait till we meet again. Sending you so much love.
Erica

That letter did not carry a lot of guilt, but what it did do was release my negative feelings towards her dying. It was honest and direct, and since my mother is buried in Texas, I can read this letter in nature, or in a quiet room, or in any place where I could feel I could connect with my mother.

I wrote the following letter to my father. My father died of cirrhosis of the liver when I was twenty-seven years old, so there was some guilt that I carried regarding my father.

Dear Dad,

I am so sorry for all the trouble I gave you growing up. I apologize for the disrespect I have caused you. I did not understand the disease of alcoholism like I do today. I am so grateful for your love, and for your sacrifice in taking care of me and my siblings. I am thankful that you fought for custody of us, and that you raised us the best you could. I am sorry for my angry feelings towards you, and for my mischievous misdeeds. I thought I knew it all, and I had nothing to learn from you, and I was terribly wrong. I want to thank you for never giving up on me, and always being there for me to the capacity that you were able to. I know today how hard life was for you, and how difficult it is to let go of alcoholism. I am ten years sober, so I know the battle of being free of alcoholism. I was wrong in my behavior towards you Dad, and I want to thank you so much for never quitting on me, and always believing in me. Thank you for coming to the births of both of my children. I am so grateful you were there. Thank you for your love, and I am so grateful that you were my father. I love you, and thank you for always watching over me, and all your grandkids. Thank you for the

moments you wrapped your love around my heart.
Love,
Erica

These two letters could be read out loud, but it would be good to do a meditation and clear your mind and call the essence of your loved one to you. It is almost like calling them to tell them all your feelings and to bare your soul to them. At the end of everything, our loved ones are filled with love, and they want us to be happy and relish in the love we have for them and the love they have for us. No matter what conflicts or problems may have occurred between you both, at the end there is always love. Do not carry guilt because your loved one does not want you to hold on to unnecessary pain. They are fine where they are at, they have peace, and they want you to have the same peace.

If you have not forgiven them, there are exercises that you can do to set yourself free. Not forgiving is very detrimental to your life. When you do not forgive, you carry all the hurt and the pain that the person left you and you are choosing to carry this big garbage bag of resentments and still trying to live your life. It is impossible for you to live an emotionally free and peaceful life if you carry a garbage bag of emotional resentments. You cannot and will not find peace.

Forgiveness is a process, and you must enter that process with any loved one, if you hope to set yourself free from the past and the pain. There was a story of a woman who grew up with her brother in a very dysfunctional home. She, in her adult life became a psychologist to try and understand the process of healing, and to heal herself as well. Unfortunately, her brother chose a destructive path. He was an alcoholic and drug abuser, and he struggled to live life in an effective manner. He had a wife and children, and when he was separating from his wife, he chose to end his life. This was traumatic and difficult for the sister, and she felt guilty because the brother called her angry the last time, she talked to him, and she tried to be supportive, but he was angry and hung up on her. She did not realize it was the last time she would ever talk to him. Later, things were moving on the cupboards, and she sensed it was her brother. She took this opportunity to learn how to connect with her brother and communicate with him. She realized he was fine, and that he finally had peace. He was trying to communicate with her and tell her that he was fine and not to feel guilty. She eventually became a medium, and she stated that her brother opened that door to this new world of mediumship. She developed a closer loving relationship with her brother after he passed, better than the one she had with him in real life.

Our loved ones want us to feel love, and they want us to have peace, so whatever unresolved issues you may have with your loved ones, you can still resolve them even though they are in spirit. If you regret not seeing them enough in their lifetime, then connect with them more often. If you need to apologize, then apologize and they will hear you. If you need to forgive them, then enter the process of forgiveness, so you can have peace. If you did not take that trip, you always wanted to take with them, then you take that trip and invite their essence in. Just because a person dies does not mean you cannot take care of unfinished business with them.

We are never alone

One of the most important things to do when you are connected with spirits or loved ones is to ground yourself. These exercises are important because you need to have a clear space, and clear energy when connecting with spirits. Once you begin connecting with a spirit, you might have other spirits that want to connect with you. It is very important that you ground yourself, and that you set very clear boundaries with spirits because you are human and you need to sleep and eat, and at times our loved ones want to connect twenty four seven, so it is up to you to say I am not open right now with conviction.

It is important to understand that you are the one with the power. These spirits are in another realm, and they cannot harm you, and you can send them away if you do not want them around. It is important not to be afraid. You must have peace when you connect with your loved ones. Fear is a negative emotion, and you may attract other spirits that you do not want because of that energy. Trust that you are loved, and you are protected, and your loved ones are with you always. If you are afraid, then do not connect with your loved ones through meditation. There are other ways to logically connect, and you do not have to feel their essence, but if you want to feel their love wrapped around you, then you must ground yourself first then meditate.

The way you ground is very simple. There are many YouTube videos that you can look up to do grounding exercises, but what I basically do to ground myself is that I close my eyes and I put my arms around myself, and I say whatever energy or love or goodness that belongs to me stay with me, but whatever energy or bad intention that is not mine go with God. I say that over and over until I feel my intuition saying I am well grounded. Another thing I do is I picture myself as an old tree, and I see roots under my feet dug deep into the ground, and I picture my hands open like tree branches. I feel strong and solid as a tree, and I say the same mantra as before: whatever belongs to me stays with me, and whatever does not go with God. Grounding is so important when connecting with our loved ones.

Meditation is the best way to connect with our loved ones. It does take practice and it is difficult to accept our random thoughts, but with practice you can master meditation. When you are meditating and you are thinking about what to have for lunch, just let the thoughts come and then release them and go back to meditating. It takes practice and you can do meditation from five to ten minutes. It does not have to be 30 minutes or an hour. You can meditate for that long, but in so many cases people say I cannot meditate, but you can always meditate because everyone has five minutes in a day. The problem is that it is a matter of priority. People make time for what is important, and if meditation is important, you will make time for it. It is up to you, the more you meditate the more you will be able to connect to the spiritual realm and the more you will be able to feel your loved ones. You can start off slow and make a commitment to yourself that you will meditate five minutes a day for a week, and once you reach that goal you make it two weeks and then three weeks, and so on. Once you do it for twenty-one days, it can become part of your routine. Many successful people meditate, and it can not only help you connect with loved ones, but it can help you slow down and clear your mind. Meditation is a powerful tool because above all it can give you peace, and peace and calm are what we all should have.

Another way to connect with our loved ones is to call on them when we need them. Our loved ones are with us and at times they will show us signs when we need to know they are near. This woman went into a bar, and she was having a rough day. She had lost the love of her life six months prior, and she was feeling down. She was upset that he was not around to comfort her on this rough day because he was always the one that helped her through rough days, and he was always there for her. Then she thought, "Where are you? Why aren't you here?" Then suddenly, she looks up at the screen, and a man is wearing a shirt with the name of her loved one. What are the odds of her asking this question, and suddenly, she sees his name on the shirt on the television. That is not a coincidence. That is her loved one saying I am here, I am always here, and I have always been here.

For years, I wanted to be able to connect to my mother since I lost her so young. I wanted to hear her words, and what she would say to me if she had a chance to speak to me. I never knew that I did not have to go to a medium to communicate with her. There were exercises I could do to connect with her. Do not get me wrong, there are some mediums that are amazing, and they have a direct line to our loved ones. As a medium, you cannot always bring through the person that your sitter wants, the spirit who wants to come through is the one that comes through. But you can always connect with them by yourself, and talk to them, and feel them around you.

My son was having a hard time, and I was really worried about him. He was living on his own, and away from me. One night my mother came to me in the middle of the night. I could feel her presence, and I could almost see her face, and she said to me," take care of your son." I knew who she was talking about because I was worried about that same son. So, I paid for my son to have a reading with a renowned medium. The reading was supposed to be in August, and we were in March. I knew it was months away, but I asked my mother to help me watch over my son.

In the month of May, things began to shift for my son because it turned out that he had his, now wife, pregnant. My son was scared to tell me, and I have to say, I handled it very well. I just told them both that a child is a blessing, and I would pray for them to figure things out. They had already decided to keep my little princess, and I was so grateful for that decision. My son was so proud of the fact that the moment they both knew it was no question that they were going to keep my little princess. I knew that this child would change both their lives, and I am beyond proud of my son as a father. You see I feel like my mother helped bring this little girl into this world because she was worried about him, and she knew this baby would change his life for the better.

Maybe she had to advocate and ask God, but I just know in my heart that my mom had something to do with this beautiful blessing in my life. Later, when he had the reading the medium mentioned that the baby. That reading really helped my son heal, and it helped him connect with his grandfather. My son is very stoic, and he rarely cries, but when he left that reading, he said he felt my dad, and he teared up because he felt his love. Our loved ones are pure love, and they love us dearly. They want us to have a great life, and they want us to feel their love.

My daughter has always had a strong connection with my father, and when she found out that my son connected with my dad, she was hurt and angry. My daughter has an intellectual disability, so she can be sensitive at times. She told me with tears in her eyes, "you know how much I love and miss my grandfather, and you could not send me." The reading itself was really expensive, so I did not even consider sending her, so I said, "the medium is going to have a group event with hundreds of people, and we can try and see if he chooses you and maybe your grandfather may give you a message." When it is a group reading, there is a slim chance that you will be chosen. One of the things the medium said was pay attention to the signs. He told a story about a woman who lost her husband on 911, and that every September 11 she finds coins on her bed. The lady then asks, is that her husband? The medium says, "of course, it is your husband, he is saying hello." Well, we stayed for the entire show, and we did not get chosen. As we were walking to the parking lot, my daughter was livid, and she said, "I came, I was here, and where was my grandpa? Where was he?" I said sometimes spirits are shy and would rather come privately. Then she said, "no, he was supposed to be there." Then suddenly on her phone, an old photo booth picture of my father pops up. It was an old picture, and it just came up on her screen and all of a sudden, I said, "here, there is your grandpa, he is here." My daughter likes to disagree, and she said, "no," but deep down it was a sign from her grandfather saying, "I am here, and I love you."

Our loved ones are filled with love, and if you need to ask for forgiveness, or say sorry there are ways you can do that. You can write them letters, or you can make time to spend with them. You can communicate with them with your thoughts. It is important that you find peace with your loved ones because they want you to be happy. They do not want you to be carrying guilt or feeling bad because you did not do or say something while they were living. Where loved ones are, they are wrapped in real authentic love, and they are so grateful that they have you to love, and they want you to be happy and emotionally free.

Signs are Everywhere

Our loved ones are advocating for us, and they want us to know that they are always nearby. They come to us when we really need a sign, or they come to us when we are down. They are there when we must make a major decision, or when we are unsure about how we are feeling about our decisions. Our loved ones are supporting us from the other side. They are with us every step of the way. They sometimes bring lovers our way, they guide us in difficult times, or they may send us pets. They are there when we are going through a crisis or when they need to feel our love.

In order for us to pay attention to the signs of our loved ones we have to be open to receiving. The problem once again is that our logical mind questions the signs, and we discount the messages as coincidences. It is like our loved ones keep knocking on our door, but we do not let them in. We must allow these messages in, and we must be aware of them happening. When our loved ones communicate with us, they can communicate through different signs. One of the most common signs our loved one's use is feathers. I am not sure why, but so many people that have come across their loved ones have found a feather. These feathers come randomly and in weird or abnormal places.

My friend lost her father due to cancer. When she spoke to him last, she reminded him to please come and try to visit her if possible. Her father died, and although it was sad for her, she hoped that he would come visit. You can do this, if you know someone is going to die, you can ask them to come and give you signs. You can ask them for specific signs. So, my friend was in her kitchen, and suddenly, she looked at the floor and saw this gray and white long feather. She knew that her father was saying hello. She then began to talk to him out loud and said hello Dad. Then later, on another night there were all these lights flashing in her house, and she realized it was her dad again. So, remember that our loved ones leave feathers as a sign of their love and their presence. I also have another friend who was connected with her father, and she found a feather on her bedroom floor. She knew it was her father saying, "I love you, and I am here." Please do not let other people's logical minds tell you something different. If a feather comes into your home, or even if you find it outside it is your loved ones saying I am here, and I love you. If you live on a bird or chicken farm, well that is a different story. However, if a feather comes randomly or you do not normally see feathers, then it is a message from your loved one saying I love you.

Sometimes we want complicated or intricate messages, but a lot of the time they just want to make their love and presence known. What you can do if you find a feather, and you want to know if your loved one has a message; you can ask them for a message, or you can ask them if they have a message? Now, what if you find a feather and you do not know who it is from, then you ask, and listen to your instinct. The first person that comes to your mind is who it is. If you want to hear their message, then stop, clear your mind and meditate and ask if they have a message, and whatever comes to your mind that is the message. If nothing comes to your mind, then they just want to show you love and they want you to feel their presence. They want to say you are never alone, and that their love and essence pervades time and space. They follow your life, and they are with you in your struggles, but above all, they believe in you, and they have faith that you will make it through. Our loved ones are our biggest advocates, and they want us to know that with their unconditional love we can get through anything.

Our loved ones connect with us through electronic devices. As I shared before, my friend's father would turn the lights on and off to show that he was there. In other cases, our loved ones could turn on the television, the radio, the windshield wipers, or they can light up your cell phone. My fiancé had a strange experience. He had a video pop up on his phone that his uncle was filming with a camcorder, and his father was in that video. There was no way for him to have had access to that video, but there it was. That video was a message to my fiancé, saying I am here, I love you, and I am with you.

In another case my friend had a voicemail from her father, and it was strange because he was not alive when she had that number, but she could hear his voice saying hello. The voice is just saying in Spanish "*Hola*" and then it cuts out. She knew it was her father, and she was shocked and surprised that her father could leave her a voicemail just saying hello. Her father was calling to say hello, I am here, and I love you.

Sometimes you are listening to the radio and suddenly, a song comes on and it reminds you of your loved one; that is them communicating with you. The song's meaning or message could be a message from your loved one because they can trigger memories long lost. Songs are magical because it is our loved ones reminding us of those moments when time was spent listening to that music. Depending on the song, it can also be a message to us. We can know this by listening to our instinct and the thoughts that come into our mind at that moment. When our loved ones communicate, they come to our thoughts, and we must trust the message. Another way my loved ones have communicated with me is through YouTube. I sometimes get suggestions from YouTube and sometimes instinctively I know it is from a loved one. So, I meditate, and I know at that moment I listen to the song suggestion and feel the essence of my loved one, and I know it is them showing me love.

A few years ago, I saw a Facebook message that my high school boyfriend had passed away. I had just messaged him to ask him a question about the Covid vaccine because he was a doctor. I had no idea there was anything wrong with him. I felt numb because I did not expect the news, and because someone that I had loved so deeply when I was young had died. I felt sadness for his three children, and the widow he was leaving behind. As I was thinking about him, YouTube popped up on my phone and began playing "The One That Got Away." I didn't even know that song existed. Did he get away because he died? Or did he get away because we lost each other years ago? I could not help but laugh. As I continued to drive, I saw his initials RC as the name of a barbershop. I had passed by that street countless times, and I had never noticed that barbershop. I pulled over to a park, and I just sat by myself and cried. When I finally got up, and walked to my car, I saw a feather, and I knew it was him saying I am here, if you ever need me, I am here.

Our loved ones want to tell us they remember the moments we spent with them, they want us to know they are with us, and they want us to listen to the music they love. One time my friend turned on her father's favorite music and she was relishing in the moment and the music. Then suddenly, she realized that she needed to get on a Zoom call, and she had to turn the music off. She turned off the music, and tried to log on to Zoom, and she kept getting kicked out. She wanted to blame the Wi-Fi, but she did not stop getting kicked out until she turned the music back on. Her father was saying no, do not turn off the music because he blocked her from staying logged into the Zoom. So, until she turned on the music, she was able to stay logged on. Her father was saying, I am here, I love you, and I love when you listen to my music.

I once lived in an apartment where a man who had cancer died. We had so many messages from this man. Even though he was not our loved one, in a way he was. My daughter was two years old, and she would say, mommy there is a man there. I did not realize that she was referring to this man. Now, I know the message he was sending to me whereas when I was young, I did not realize it. I just thought it was a spirit who was still in his apartment. I did not think that he was trying to give me a message. My ex-husband and I had an old TV that did not have a remote control, and that TV would turn on and off at random times. Now as I reflect, I realize that the TV would go on when my ex-husband and I were arguing, or when we were at odds, or when there was negative heavy energy in the home. My ex-husband and I had a very toxic relationship, and the emotional energy in the house was harsh, so in retrospect I think this spirit was trying to tell us to stop wasting time arguing, stop being angry, and that life is too short. People who have died do not want us to make the same mistakes they made in life. That is why they want us to take risks and live fearlessly because they do not want us to waste our time letting our emotions take joy from our life. One of the best skills a person can develop is to learn how to manage their emotions because this is key to finding your way to joy. You are going to have problems, and life is going to hit you hard at times, but it is so important you manage your emotions effectively. I am not saying to numb your emotions or to keep yourself so busy that you cannot feel your emotions. What I mean is to lean into your feelings and ask your higher self what message these feelings are supposed to tell you, and then thank your feelings for the message, and release them.

Our loved ones often leave coins lying around in unexpected places. I have heard so many stories of people finding coins. They happen to find these coins on anniversaries, birthdays, or on a day when you are dealing with something difficult. It is your loved one saying I am here, and I see you. I know life can be hard, and sometimes we feel like we are so alone, but during these times our loved ones are listening, and they are there, we just have to be aware of these signs. Sometimes we can be so overwhelmed that we miss the signs, and these signs are so important because it is a hug, a kiss, a sign of their love, and they are saying you are not alone. Coins can come as you are walking down the street, and that could be your loved one. Again, if you do not know whose coin it is, ask, and follow your intuition.

My father held on to change for dear life. He had a jar of coins that he always had filled. My father even collected old coins because he believed that one day those coins would have some value. My sister would call him the *King of Change* because he had coins everywhere. He had change in every single drawer, in his pockets, all over his truck, in the cushions of the sofa, and on the counters. He was the type of person who would rather have change than have dollars. I think that in his mind he would spend dollars faster, so my father held on to change. One time my sister and I needed two dollars to go to the movies and we paid with loose pennies for both our tickets because we took our dad's change. Another time my sister came to work in the city I live in, and since she stayed for almost two weeks, I would wash her laundry, so she would not have to go to the laundromat. In her clothes, I found two nickels in two different loads. I brought the nickels back to her room, and said here is your change, and she said, that change is not mine. We both looked at each other, and she said, "it is my dad." That was his message to us. He knew we were together, and he was grateful that I was there for her in such a simple way as washing her laundry.

Another way loved ones communicate is through smells. My father was an alcoholic, and he always worked hard labor, and after work he would drink a beer, he would smell like that sweaty beer smell. He would also always drink coffee in the morning, and so in the morning my father would always smell like coffee. My father knew

31

he was going to die. He knew he was suffering from cirrhosis of the liver, and he was very sick at times. However, he did not want to die. On his deathbed, he kept saying take me home. My father lived with my brother, and my brother said he could not handle us taking my father home, so we stayed around him in the hospital and laughed at memories and prayed. We did not want our father to die, but his body was failing, and it was time for him to go. He once told me that he was going to come back, and he was going to visit me. One of the first times he visited, I could tell, because I could smell him. I was driving home and suddenly that sweaty beer smell appeared, and I knew at that moment it was my father. He was there, and he was with me like he promised.

My sister lived in Vegas when my father died. My sister did not even own a coffee maker. When she left Texas to return home, she felt my dad's presence. The day after she arrived from Texas, her husband woke up, and she woke up soon after. My sister looked at her husband and said, "I smell coffee." She was looking at him like he was getting up before her and bringing coffee, and her husband responded, "I smell coffee too," and that is when tears began streaming down her face and she said, "it's my dad." It was my father telling her I am here, and you are not alone. Another time I was with my middle brother, and we both got in the car and looked at each other, and I said do you smell that, and he said yes, it is dad. I said, "Hi dad." Our loved ones come to us through smells. Another friend of mine lost her husband to cancer, and her husband would be around smokers and he would come home smelling like cigarettes even though he never smoked. When he died, my friend would always know it was her husband when she would smell cigarette smoke with no one smoking. She knew her husband was saying hello, I am here, and I love you.

My father also told me that he would make sounds or drop a cup to communicate with me. It is as if he knew he could come back and show his presence. My father had a very distinct whistle. I was once in a mall, and I heard my dad's whistle. I was looking frantically around to see where it was coming from, and I could not determine where, I then realized it was my father. I had never heard anyone whistle like my father, but I knew at that moment it was him. Sometimes you can hear your loved ones laugh, their voice, or even an activity they always did. For example, if your loved one always did the lawn and you hear a lawn mower and it reminds you of him/her, then it is him/her. Sounds that remind you of your loved ones indicate their presence. Another example could be a leaf blower, a rake, a drill, or the sound of a sewing machine. If these sounds are associated with your loved one, it is them telling you I am here and remember when I did this or that.

Other signs can be found in pictures. For example, orbs, rays of light, or faces can all be seen in pictures. There are countless stories of people seeing light, orbs, or faces in pictures but they discount these images as coming from the camera or scenery. I had mentioned before that our loved ones can interfere with electronic devices, and they can be captured in pictures. I know many non-believers think that these pictures are photo shopped, or computer generated, but in my experience many of these pictures are legitimate signs of our loved ones. I knew a woman who was getting married, and she was sad that her mother had passed before her wedding. In so many of her pictures there were rays of light coming down and engulfing the couple. These rays of lights and orbs were a sign from her mother saying I was there, and I did not miss it. She was showing her love to the new couple through the pictures. Please do not discount rays of light or orbs in pictures. These phenomena are messages from our loved ones saying I am here, I love you, and I remember you.

Another thing that shows in pictures are faces in objects or shadows. These pictures can reflect the faces of our loved ones, and they are being captured in the pictures as proof of their presence. When you take the picture, it is like they are saying hello to you, I am here. These pictures can be seen in the outline of clouds, trees, objects, or it can be a shadow of their body frame. It is them saying I see you, and I remember you. Losing a loved one can be hard, but you can find peace and consolation in that they say hello in your pictures through orbs and rays of light.

Rainbows are another way our loved ones come through to show us love. I have a friend who recently moved to Statesboro, Georgia. They were purchasing a new home, and her husband's father had just passed away. It was a lot of change for them in a short period of time. The home they were coming to had to have a new pool installed, and the whole move and the recent death had them both on edge. Then suddenly they both looked up and they saw this beautiful rainbow in the sky, they both felt that it was the husband's father, and she also felt her mother's presence. It gave them the security that they were making the right choice in moving, and they felt that both his dad and her mom were looking over them. Our loved ones can come in rainbows on anniversaries, birthdays, or when you feel desperate.

Lastly, another common way our loved ones come to us is through nature. Sometimes we can take a walk in nature and connect with them in that way. Sometimes unexpectedly we see a bird chirping and it catches our attention, and we get a feeling that it is our loved one. In other cases, it could be an exotic bird that is not common in your area, and that could be your loved one. I have heard people say they saw a blue jay, mockingbird, and cardinal and they knew that it was their loved one connecting to them. You have to listen to your intuition and if you do not know who it is, then ask and you will get the answer in your thoughts and in your gut. I personally believe that all hummingbirds are our loved ones visiting us and sending us a bit of love.

Butterflies are another way loved ones communicate. Butterflies are so random, and they can come at different times and places. Butterflies are symbols of both beauty and love. For me personally, butterflies have come to me in times where I was feeling overwhelmed and lost. All of a sudden, a butterfly would cross my path, and I knew that it was either my father or my mother. I heard a story of a woman who was moving from her first family home. She lost her daughter to cancer, and she knew it was the best for her family, but she felt the guilt of leaving the last home her daughter lived in. They finally accepted an offer from a younger person who was expecting a child. The woman knew that the time in her first family home was going to end soon. Her windows were open, and suddenly, a beautiful butterfly came in and flew around her, and her husband. The butterfly flew all over the room and all around them. Then suddenly, a tiny little feather flew on the husband's shirt. The butterfly eventually left, and the husband and wife knew that their daughter was giving them her blessing to sell the house.

In another story, a man was sitting on a rock by a river waiting to hear of the death of a friend that was approaching. He did not want to be with the friend at the moment of his death, and he just wanted to be alone on this rock till he heard that he was gone. Suddenly, he saw this beautiful monarch butterfly that was flying near the brush. It was weird because there were no flowers to attract the butterfly there, and yet it stood there for what seemed like a long time. He knew at that point, his friend was gone, and he knew his friend came and said good-bye through the presence of that butterfly.

Another way our loved ones come to us is through ladybugs. Ladybugs come at random times and in random places as well. These bugs are so cute, and it is amazing that these little creatures can represent our loved ones. My sister was having a conversation with her husband about the way our loved ones communicate with us, and they both were talking about ladybugs. They both were saying that ladybugs are a way that our loved ones connect with us. My grandmother had just passed, and they were commenting that they wondered how my grandmother was going to connect with them. The next day there was a windstorm and they had to remove the canopy, and suddenly, a ladybug landed on my sister, and it stayed with her for a long time. She knew it was our grandmother, and she was so grateful she had the opportunity to connect with her.

As stated before, the more you practice meditation, the more you connect with your intuition, the easier it is for you to connect with your loved ones. Be aware of all these signs that are available to you. When you have a heightened awareness of these signs, you will be surprised at how often our loved ones connect with us. There are so many signs around us, and just know that your loved ones are with you, and they are saying I am here, and I love you.

Sing, Dance, Listen, Watch

Most of the time our loved ones liked music or a show that is associated with a theme song. It could be a song that you associate with your loved one, or a theme song that reminds you of them. You can create a playlist of all the songs that remind you of your loved one, or you could play a full album of the songs that your loved one loved. You can always meditate, connect and call upon your loved one as you relish in the moment and listen to his/her favorite musician or band. They enjoy listening to the music with you. You can even dance because they love to see you rejoice in the moment.

As mentioned before, if you use YouTube, and you listen to music that reminds you of your loved one, YouTube often gives you suggestions of songs daily, and those songs can come from your loved ones. Sometimes there are songs that you did not even know existed, but those songs are meant for you to hear from your loved one. Again, if you are not sure which loved one it is, you can always ask who this is from, and your first instinct or your first thought is who it is trying to connect with you.

When you get suggestions, listen to all aspects of the song because their message could be in the lyrics, or it can be in the melody of the song. Pay attention to the title of the song because sometimes just the title is your message. When you listen to the playlist that you create from your loved one, YouTube will automatically make suggestions, those suggestions are songs sent to you by your loved ones. With those songs they are saying hello, I am thinking of you, and I love you, so I am sending you this song.

If you spend countless hours listening to music with your loved one, understand that this will probably be the best way for them to connect with you. You can visualize or meditate on those moments you spent with them listening to certain songs. If you went to concerts with them, or music festivals you can always invite your loved one to go with you to a concert and you could feel their presence. Remember that most of the time they communicate in your thoughts, so whatever thoughts come to your mind as you are preparing for the day it is their commentary saying this is my opinion about this or that. Personalities of our loved ones do not change; if you could hear your loved one cracking a joke, being sarcastic, or being dramatic, that is because they are saying those things in spirit.

I had a couple of friends from high school who passed away. One I had no idea he had passed. I found out three years later, and I felt such sadness when I found out because had I known I would have made the trip to pay my condolences. Frankie was such a great friend, and such an amazing man. He died in a car accident, and his death was sudden. I really wished I had a chance to tell him how much he meant to me, and that I was beyond grateful for his friendship. He was that guy in high school who would always make you smile because he always had something to say. On my way back home, I was walking through the airport and a really old song was playing that came out when we were in high school. The song was, "More than words" by Extreme. It was the perfect song, because the part of the lyrics basically said you do not have to say I love you because I know already, and I was sad but at peace because he knew I loved him.

I knew at that moment he was talking to me. He knew that I loved him, and that I did not have to say those words because he knew. He knew that if I had known I would have gone to the funeral, and that he was grateful for my friendship as much as I was grateful for him. It was sad that we lost touch, but those high school moments we shared being friends can never be taken away from us. I loved him so very much, and he knew it. I did not have to say the words, and I did not have to go to his funeral because no matter what he knew I loved him. I heard him in my thoughts, "It was my job to keep you smiling and happy, and I would not have wanted to see you crying and sad at my funeral." I had closure and peace because of the song he sent me, and I was beyond grateful for it.

In the middle of writing this book my cousin James Castro died. They found him in his home, and he was unresponsive. He had diabetes, and the cause of his death is unclear because the details are not consistent. All I know is that he was found by the people who were supposed to take him to dialysis because he lived alone. I was in my classroom when I received the phone call about his death. I felt like the wind was knocked out of me. I was supposed to see him the following week at a *quinceanera*. I had an opportunity to see him on June 13, 2021, because he just so happened to be in El Paso, and we spent a day together. I was talking to my students about my book and how we could connect with our loved ones, and I said I am going to ask my cousin for a sign, and I said a bird.

I felt numb and sick to my stomach, but I had things to do, and as I went to get some food to eat, my daughter said look there is a bird on that car. I knew at that moment my cousin was giving me a sign. This loss was great for me because he took care of my sister and me when we were small, and he cared about us so much. I did not talk to him very often, but the love I had for him was tremendous. I loved him so much, and so I had to go through this grieving process during the creation of the book.

I came to work on Monday, and I got a suggestion from YouTube. It was a song by Brent Morgan, *I got you*, I know that was the song he was sending me because it was like I am here for you, and I love you. I know it is a romantic song, and for us it was a song for cousins, and I know it is hard, and I have been crying all these days because I lost my cousin, but I know that no matter where he is, he is watching out for me.

On the day of my cousin's funeral, I could not attend. I live in California, and my cousin's funeral was going to be in Sanderson, Texas. There is no airport to Sanderson, the closest airport was two hours and forty minutes away. I was somewhat sad because I could not attend. I was aware of the time of his funeral, I meditated a bit and tried to stop in the middle of my day to honor him and remember him. I know I was not there, but my heart was with him and his children. Later, as I was picking up my son from daycare, I saw a hummingbird, and I felt a sense of peace because I knew it was a message from him. I love him so much and I am beyond grateful that God chose him to be my cousin.

Another way to connect with your loved ones is to invite them to watch movies, or TV shows with you. If you are familiar with the likes and dislikes of your loved one regarding movies and shows you can invite them to spend time with you when you are watching these shows or movies. If a new movie comes out, and you feel like your loved one would love to watch that movie, then make it a date. Meditate to clear your mind, make some time and space for your loved one to come and sit by you and if a thought comes in your head of a comment they would say, that is what they are saying. For example, if there is a dumb part in the movie, and you hear in your thoughts that it's so dumb, then your loved one is expressing that thought about the movie or show. If your loved one liked a particular show, and they watched that show religiously on a weekly basis you can invite them weekly to watch that show with you. If you cannot watch it on a particular day, just record it or save it on your DVR and watch it with them when you have time or when you can.

I have a close friend that has struggled with drugs and alcohol in her life. Praise God she is doing well now, but there was a moment in her life where she got lost in the party scene because she was numbing her pain. She had an extremely controlling roommate and her boyfriend was living far away, but he was very toxic too. She was watching a movie called *A Little Chaos,* and she felt she was not alone. Her grandmother had come from the other side and wrapped her essence around her and gave her unconditional love. My friend burst into tears and began the process of releasing pain. The drama in the movie was like all the drama she was experiencing at the time, and she felt that her grandmother came to her to show her love. The movie was symbolic because it was dramatic like her life, and the character felt alone, and the grandmother came to her, to show she was loved and never alone.

Live the fullest life

Our loved ones want us to make our dreams come true. They want us to live fearless lives. So whatever dream or desire you have, they want us to create it and follow through. If you are miserable at your job, and you have always felt that you could do something more, our loved ones want us to try and take that risk. Our loved ones are like guides, and everything they did not achieve in their life, they would want us to achieve in our lives. When people pass, they have insights and realizations that we cannot have because we are living. I am assuming that they look over their life and think of how grateful they are for their life. But they probably think that they should have done all these things that they never did. I think that it is important to think about death, and to think about all the things that we want to achieve or accomplish before we die. On a separate note, it is important to take care of our wills, life insurance, and all those logistical things we must take care of before we die.

I had a friend who told me that when his father died, he felt his angry energy around him. What happened was that when the father died, he did not have all the proper paperwork, so the estate went into probate. It was too expensive to keep the house, and the best option for those still living was to sell the house. The father's energy was angry because he worked so hard to pay for the house, and he was angry that it was sold. Weeks at a time the father would come to him, and he could feel his angry energy. My friend finally figured out why he was so angry, and he finally said out loud, "Dad, if you wanted us to keep the house, then you should have done a better job securing it and doing the proper paperwork to avoid probate. My sister and I did the best we could in trying to keep it, but we could not, so I am sorry." After my friend said that his dad never became angry again. He came with a gentle, and calming energy. This is important because we all need to be responsible, and we cannot have our loved ones clean up our mess. We want our loved ones to be able to take care of our legacy and all the things we leave behind with ease. It is bad enough that they are mourning our loss, so it is important that we take care of our responsibilities and avoid having our family members go to probate if possible.

In another case, make sure you divide your assets up the way you want them to be divided up. Sometimes when people remarry, the children often do not get the things that they were promised by their loved one. I do not know why this happens, but in so many instances when someone dies there is so much conflict with who gets what, and that often happens with blended families. I have heard of so many stories where the children or grandchildren are left out because the second wife does not want to comply with the father's desires. That is why it is so important to have a will, and the assets to be divided legally. We often fail to take care of these logistics because we procrastinate, and we do not see them as important. However, the worst thing that could happen for a family is for its members to lose their relationship because a person did not set up their will and testament properly. You could do it anonymously, in that no one knows how you are dividing the assets until you pass away. This can eliminate a lot of problems with estate planning.

I was in a group reading when a man came through who wanted to apologize to his daughter because he did not take care of the logistics of his estate. Her father had remarried, and he did not leave a will and testament, so a lot of the property that he owned went to the second wife. In some states, the property acquired before the marriage does not automatically become community property, and if the property was in only his name, he could have gifted it to his daughter. He was very sorry for not properly planning, and for not leaving her the property he had intended for her and his grandkids.

On a separate note, our loved ones want us to reach great heights in our lives, and they want us to accomplish all the things we find unimaginable. All great ideas can come to life, and since in the spirit realm or in heaven there are no limitations, our loved ones want us to overcome our earthly limitations and accomplish all the crazy dreams that we have conceived in our minds. Our loved ones want to be there with us, and they want to love us and wrap their essence around us when we achieve these feats. Our loved ones do not only want to be with us when we are sad, they want to celebrate our successes as well. They get excited when we meet our soul mate, when we have our children, when we get a promotion, or any major or minor achievement.

A mother once lost her daughter to brain cancer, and this girl used to love to hike trails and climb mountains. Before her daughter died, the mother and the daughter made a pact to meet on top of a famous mountain. When the mother was asked why she was training, and preparing herself to climb this mountain, she said because "although I am scared, I promised my daughter I would, and everything I do to prepare for this climb keeps me closer to my daughter. I know that she is with me every step of the way. The harder I work and dedicate myself to accomplish this feat the closer I am to my daughter´s soul. I will always do whatever it takes for me to feel close to my daughter and if that means climbing mountains, then I will climb mountains." Create a goal your loved one would want you to achieve and take them with you.

Make a list of things that your loved one would want you to do. Brainstorm and make a list of all the things, do not really put thought into it, just write down whatever comes to mind. Just because you write it on the list, does not mean you have to do it, at this point you are just brainstorming. There needs to be joy in this process. If this feels like a chore, then you are using your right brain too much, and you are missing the point of the exercise. This is supposed to be fun, and exciting. You also have to dream big, so if one of the goals is to go to Europe, do not second guess yourself, and think you cannot afford it. Your loved ones are on your side, and what our loved ones can do in the spirit world is amazing, and if it is within God's sight for you to go to Europe, then it will happen. Do not think about how this is going to happen, think and imagine how it is going to feel when this happens.

My father was a Denver Broncos fan, and even though my daughter was raised a San Francisco 49er fan, she changed her team in high school. I believe that somehow my father influenced her in spirit to change teams, and root for his team. One day I was able to secure San Diego Charger tickets while they were playing the Broncos. My daughter was so excited that we were going to the game. Throughout the process of getting ready and driving to the stadium I thought about my father. I wished that somehow, he was there with us, and then I realized that he was. He was with us in spirit. It was a crazy game the Broncos were losing in the fourth quarter, and at the last minute they came back and won due to a field goal. I believe my dad was there, and it was his essence that brought the Broncos luck during that game.

Maybe the goal for you is to finish school. Maybe you are deciding to change careers, and you are interested in having a different life, trust that your loved one will be with you every step of the process. Maybe you want to start your own business, and you are afraid to take the leap. Know that your loved ones are rooting for you and will be with you every step of the way, so take a chance. I was in a group reading once, when this young lady in a suit came in, she must have been just 25 years old. All of a sudden, the medium mentions her grandfather's name. She gets excited, and says I knew he would be here. Basically, the grandfather came and told her to continue with her business and that she would have a breakthrough and would be successful. That the biggest mistake for her would be to go back and get a job. The medium was laughing because he said her grandfather came with a PowerPoint presentation trying to explain to the young lady that she had everything she needed to be successful in business.

In another instance a man came through and told the son not to give up on the quilt idea. Sometimes we want to create photo albums, heirlooms, quilts, or frames that represent our loved ones, but we never get around to it, so it is important that we get these commemorations done. The man's father collected shirts, and the man did not know what to do with all those shirts, until his wife suggested a quilt. The problem is that sometimes life gets in the way, and we do not make these goals a priority. Our loved ones want us to create these things, so we can commemorate them. A goal can be to create a memento to remember your loved one.

Since you have your loved one in heaven, now you have someone that can be with you no matter what choices you make. Make your list of all the things you would like to invite your loved one to do with you and keep to it. Make a bucket list and invite your loved one into those experiences so they too can relish the moment, and you can enjoy their essence.

Once you make your list, it is important to meditate and take some time and space to rank your list from what you can achieve right away, and those things that are going to take some planning. Set goals and dates for each of the items of your list and get started right away. Meditate and invite your loved ones in, as they are supporting your endeavors.

In the movie *PS. I love you*, the husband who died of brain cancer writes his wife letters to inspire her out of her depression and push her to start living her life without fear. He has a series of tasks that she must do, and she receives a letter every few days, and she has to follow through with what he asks. These letters allowed her to take risks and get out of her conservative ways. She speaks her mind and becomes aware of her mistakes. She loses her job and finds her passion in designing shoes. He sets up a trip for her with her friends to Ireland, and she does all those things on the list. She sings karaoke, and she finds herself moving through the grieving process. The most important lesson in the movie is that we need to see ourselves and love ourselves the way they love us. We must see ourselves through their eyes because when we do, we have no limits. The only limits that we have are those earthly limits that we put on ourselves. If you live your life with your loved ones in mind, you will be able to accomplish and do things that you never thought possible. Make that list, rank it, and then make it happen, but always have your loved ones in mind.

Reach out to them

One of the most successful coaches in the history for college basketball was John Wooden. He won ten NCAA championships and is the coach with the most championships in history. He was a man of great character and wisdom; he had high standards for his players. In the 70's, men had long hair, and beards, and John Wooden would not allow his players to not be clean cut. Bill Walton once told him, "I am not going to be clean cut," and John Wooden responded, "I understand how you feel, and we are sure going to miss you." Wooden was a beautiful person who believed in the importance of character. This is important because this man loved one woman, his beautiful wife Nell, and she died on May 21, 1985. His wife was the only woman he dated, and she was the woman of his life. He lived his life honoring his wife every 21st of the month. He would go to the grave site and write her a letter every month to tell her how excited he was to see her once again. Nell died at age 73, and John Wooden died at age 98, and he kept up those letters until he died. He would also sleep only on his side of the bed, and he would have her letters on her pillow.

Our loved ones are still there, and we can connect with them through writing letters. They love it when we celebrate birthdays or death anniversaries. It could be beautiful to have a journal for each loved one you want to connect to and write them letters. Sometimes we think "if I could only speak to our loved one, one more time, I would say...." I encourage you to write your letter and tell your loved ones all you want to say. You can buy them cards, or celebrate any other special occasion, write them letters, and call them to be present during these times.

Writing letters can help you document the times you connect with your loved one, and you can always go back and read the letters and see how you felt at the time of writing them. This is important because sometimes the worries you had years ago may not be the worries you have today. Just venting to your loved one helps to find solutions to problems or issues. In addition, our loved ones are looking out for us and are trying to guide us through the obstacles in our lives.

If you are forgetful, have a calendar on your phone that reminds you of the anniversaries to honor your loved ones. The letters do not have to be extravagant ten-page letters. Just the fact that you are making the time to write to your loved one is enough. The power of letters helps you express your thoughts and feelings, but it also helps you appreciate your loved one, and our loved ones are listening.

You can also do a letter writing challenge. You can make a commitment to write a letter for 30 days on let's say your birthday month, or your loved one's birthday month, or it could be to honor any anniversary. Use your instinct to determine what to honor. You can write these letters on your phones, or there are online journals that you can write your letters in. You can also write the letters in an old-fashioned journal. The point is to take the time and connect with your loved one through letters.

You can also ask your loved ones for prayers through letters. If your loved one was the person that you connected to and vented to, then you can ask your loved one for prayers asking them to pray for you and advocate for you. I think when our loved ones die, the hardest part is not having them there to guide us, or listen to our problems, so writing letters is a good way to connect with our loved ones to express all the feelings that we sometimes keep trapped inside. Letters help heal, and they help us connect, and keep our loved one's present. They are with us always, so they know all we do, and all we need from them.

Here is a letter I wrote when I unexpectedly lost a dear friend.

My dearest Sandra,

I don't quite understand what happened, and how you went so suddenly. I loved talking to you on the phone and hearing your wise words. I am so grateful that I got to know you, and I had you in my life. I love you so much my beautiful Canadian friend. Your loss has been great, and I want to say how grateful I am that you came and spoke to my students. I know you touched lives when you taught them about releasing forgiveness. I am so glad you worked one on one with my student who needed to release all that pain. I am grateful you worked with me, my brother, and one of my friends. I am so very glad you cleared our energy, and you had us release all those attachments that we had that were hindering our progress. I cannot understand why you left us so quickly, but all I can say is that I love you dearly and I will always love and remember you.

Erica

My friend, Sandra, was diagnosed with cancer and died within a week. I loved her so very much, and she was so important in my life. She made an impact on my students' lives, and she helped me and my brother, and one of my friends release those people who we still have not forgiven. I will never forget my dearest friend. She taught me so much about attachments and releasing those feelings of unforgiveness. She was extremely intuitive, but most of all she loved me unconditionally, and she accepted me fully wholly and completely. I am beyond grateful to have had her in my life for the time that I did.

The next letter I wrote to my friend from high school who passed away in a car accident. He was just 41 years old, and he died instantly. I did not find out about his death until about three years later because I live in Los Angeles, and it was only when I went to visit some friends in El Paso that they told me. I was devastated. Frankie made high school easier for me. He was friendly, kind, and loving. He always made me laugh, and we always sat next to each other because his last name was Carrasco and mine is Castro. Frankie always put a smile on my face, and his smile was infectious. I always felt comforted and accepted by Frankie. Whenever things were hard, we never talked about it, but his presence always made me feel like things were going to get better. I still, to this day, remember his phone number. I really appreciated all he did for me in high school. I wrote this letter to honor Frankie when I found out he died.

Dear Frankie,

I wish I had known of your departure. I really miss you. I know in the latter years we were not close, but I want you to remember that I enjoyed every moment I spent with you as my friend in high school.

You made my difficult life easier. I want to thank you for being there and accepting me. I want you to know that I appreciated your kindness. I still remember the day I went to see you at Kinkos, and you said I looked the same. That was the beauty of you Frankie, we could go years without talking, but when we saw each other again it was like we never stopped talking. I still have the birthday card, it was the belated card with the monkey in the front saying oops I forgot your birthday. I appreciated that you were a constant in my life back then, and when I was falling apart just your presence kept me together. Thank you so much Frankie for believing in me and supporting me during the very difficult times in high school. No matter what was going on, you would make a joke, or you would smile, and it would melt my sorrows away.

Thank you, Frankie, I will never forget you.
Erica

These are commemoration type letters, but you can write daily letters, and tell your loved one about your day. You can tell them about your problems, and the difficulties you may have in life. You can tell them about the things in life you are grateful for, and you can tell them funny stories about your life or even dramatic stories. For those of you who use a diary, or journal it can become a consistent exercise. You can write a letter to a loved one every day and share your thoughts and feelings. When you connect with them at this level, they are always listening and advocating for you to succeed in your life.

A good thing for you to do if you are choosing to write a letter to a loved one is to pray and meditate before you write. Get yourself in a serene space and feel calm. You can often ask your guides or God for guidance on what to write to your loved one. You should not overthink things. You must write everything down as it comes, and your writing must flow freely. If you get stuck because you do not know what to say, take a moment to breathe, meditate, pray, and start again by writing what comes to mind. Your letter does not have to be perfect. It just must be authentically you, honest, and humble. Once you write your letter, then call your person and say out loud I give you this letter with all the love of my soul, and just pause and feel the love and the essence of your loved one. The more you practice connecting, the more you will be able to feel and connect with your loved one. Do not forget your loved one's anniversaries, holidays, and bring them to celebrate your birthday. Write letters, and connect with them on a consistent basis, and you will be able to feel them more consistently.

Talk with them

I know living without our loved ones is very difficult, especially if they were our rock on this earth. However, we must honor them because we are living the legacy that they left behind in us. Do not feel it as a burden or a heavy responsibility, but I urge you to live your life in full swing and do those things that you have a passion for and live the happiest life possible for you, but most of all for them and the legacy you are leaving behind. In the life you are living, you are representing your ancestors and those who previously existed so that you can exist. The life you have today is generations in the making. There are generations upon generations who came before and paved the way, so you can exist. Are you doing all you can do to honor and make your ancestors proud?

When things are crazy and you feel lost, you can have a conversation with your loved one out loud and tell them everything that is going on in your life. You can pray with them out loud or tell them all the words you wanted to tell them in life and could not. You can say to your loved one "good morning," "I miss you," and "be with me." Speaking out loud and writing brings everything into reality, and it brings the words into existence. Talking out loud to speak to our loved ones helps our loved ones understand how we feel. It helps them understand that we need them and that we keep them present in our lives.

Talking out loud to our loved ones also releases energy from our bodies because we are venting and releasing our emotions. We are releasing our thoughts, and we are releasing all the words that we have been holding on to. You can call your loved one in and practice a speech, or a pitch, or a presentation that you might have to do for work. It is very important that we connect with our loved ones by talking out loud because it makes them more involved in our lives and it works for their essence to come forth more often. When you practice connecting with your loved one, it will become second nature, and you will be able to connect easier as you continue to practice.

One time my sister came to work in the city I lived in, and since I had not seen her for over two years, I made an effort to see her on a daily basis even though she was staying about forty-five minutes away. My brother also came into town, and one time my brother was supposed to pick her up at eleven in the morning. I was getting out of work at eleven in the morning, so I had no idea my sister was waiting and angry, and she was declining calls. When I found out she was waiting, I left right away, and I was talking out loud to both my parents telling them, "Please control and calm your daughter." This was an opportunity for us three to be together. I asked, "Mom and dad please calm her, and change her mind to come with us." When I called my sister, she answered, but she was angry, and I explained to her what happened, and she told me to wait for her there. I know my sister when she gets angry it takes her awhile for her to calm down, but I knew that me speaking to my parents out loud would help her calm down before I got there.

When I lose someone I love and my emotions are all over the place, I talk with them out loud. At other times, when I miss someone I love, I speak out loud the words I need to release and need them to hear. Sometimes we do not get the opportunity to tell someone how much they meant in our lives, and the impact they left on our hearts, and when I feel the pang of sadness, I talk with them out loud. Even when I am angry and hurt that they died, I ask why out loud. It does not fail, after I speak or scream out loud to my loved ones, I feel a sense of calmness and peace.

People are sometimes in your life for a short time, but even then, they make an impact. I had an ex-boyfriend from high school who believed in me more than I believed in myself. Although we lost touch, and I moved west and he stayed in Texas, I was always grateful that his belief in me, led me to believe in myself. In high school, I took Trigonometry, Calculus, Physics, and Analytical Geometry because he believed I could succeed. We were not together in our senior year, but it was because of him that I was able to get into those classes and succeed. Those classes were hard for me. I was not a math person, but I was grateful that he had faith in me when I signed up for them. Later, in college we became acquaintances, and he knew I had low self-esteem and he told me to look in the mirror and say I love you to myself. I thought he was crazy, who would do that? Who would look in the mirror and say I love you, and he said, "mean it when you say it." I was grateful for the short time he was in my life, and the impact he made. When he died, I felt like there was so much I wish I would have said to him. I had no idea that he would die. In my mind, I always thought I would see him at a reunion or something, but he died, and I handled all the words that I did not say to him by talking to him out loud. I said, "thank you for believing in me and challenging me to take those difficult courses." I told him, "Thank you so much for teaching me to say I love you to myself and thank you for making me better." Even in the short time I had him in my life, I felt peace telling him all the things I would have liked to say in life by speaking to him out loud.

You can even write a speech to honor your loved one and say it out loud. They hear every word you say to them. I had a speaking competition, and the theme was fathers. I planned to go to my father's grave site in Texas, carry his picture, and do my speech in honor of my father and record it. In it, I talked about how my father was the rock that built me, and how he loved us. When my mother died, he almost lost custody of us four kids because he was an alcoholic, but my father fought to keep us. He did everything he could to keep us together. Although the turmoil of alcohol made it difficult to live a happy childhood, my father loved us above all. I carried a lot of pain and resentment towards my father in my lifetime, but there was a beautiful moment that I witnessed with my father that dissipated all the hurt and pain. When my daughter was three years old, my daughter would grab my father's stump because he lost his leg due to an infection, and I was standing by the door out of sight. I could see my daughter laughing and playing with my dad creating a priceless memory. The love my father had for his grandkids was unparalleled. He loved them so much, and these kids never saw my father drunk. I got the biggest gift of my life in witnessing my father sober for the last three years of his life. His illnesses no longer allowed him to drink, and man did I meet a man that was charming, funny, charismatic, and full of love. It did not matter how he started his life, my father finished strong because he left some deep memories in his grandkids, and my daughter to this day celebrates him and has his picture in her room. For the last five years, my daughter has bought a cake for my father, and we all sing him happy birthday. This speech was so healing for me because it described a man that although alcoholic left a legacy of love through his children and his grandkids.

Lastly, I had an uncle and aunt that died when I was thirteen years old. I loved them both very much. They both died in a car accident together, and they were both there for me and my siblings when my mother died. As a matter of fact, they took all four of us to Sanderson, Texas, for the summer so my father could recover from my mother's death. My father struggled with my mother's death, so my aunt and uncle both volunteered to take us in for a few months before school started. My aunt Adelina and I had the same birthday, so she had a special love for me. She took me to all kinds of places. She was always driving around town, she loved to play bingo, and she loved spending time with me. When I was about ten years old, we were driving and she told me, "I want you to succeed. I want you to go to school and do something with your life. You are smart, and I know you have everything you need to succeed." At that point in my life, I was struggling in school. I did not take school seriously, and I was very distracted in my work. When she told me that I felt a renewed sense of trying, and the fact that my current teacher did not believe in me added fuel to the fire. I was not trying my best, so I tried, and I almost made the honor roll, but the following year I did well, and continued to do so. My aunt told me, "Go to my grave and show me all the things you have done and show me your degrees and awards." I do not know how she knew that she would be gone so soon, but she did. In 2017, I did just that. I took my son who was a few months old, I took my niece, and I found my uncle and aunt's grave, and I said, "thank you for loving me and believing in me. I did it. I went to school, and I got two degrees. I am a teacher, and I made something of myself because of you." I was so humbled and emotional as I stood there and told them my life story, and how grateful I was for them and everything they did for me and my siblings. When you talk out loud with your loved ones they listen.

At any point in your life, always remember that you can always talk to your loved ones out loud. They hear you, they are with you, and they love you. No matter what is happening, your loved ones are always there ready to listen.

Stay Grateful

The hardest thing about losing a loved one is that it makes it very difficult to stay in gratitude. When we lose a loved one, we feel like victims because it hurts so much, and what makes it more difficult is that we do not have the answer as to why. Even when our loved one is sick, it is still difficult to make peace with their death and let our loved one go. Our emotions are so tied to them, and the love we share with our loved ones transcends time and space. Even though we know they are with us, it is very difficult to stay in gratitude especially through the grieving process.

The grieving process is hard, and it comes in waves, but as much as you can I want you to remember stories that made you laugh, or moments that you are grateful for which were spent with your loved one. Remember the happy moments, or those moments that you will never forget. Our loved ones are precious gems that impacted our lives, made us who we are, and touched our lives in ways that we could not have imagined. There are behaviors or sayings that we can remember saying out loud.

When my siblings and I get together, that is what we do. We repeat sayings that our father, grandfather, and even our uncle said in the past. We also tell stories about our father that used to make us laugh. All of us would love to have one more moment with my father, but when we tell these stories, and we laugh, these are the memories that keep our loved one alive, and we can get into gratitude.

We sometimes hear stories that we did not even know happened. My middle brother recently told me a story when he had to pick up my dad from a meeting in downtown El Paso, Texas. When my brother pulled up, he quickly parked the car because the police were frisking my dad. My brother goes up to the police, and says, "hey, what are you guys doing?" The police respond by telling my brother to stand up against the wall, and they start frisking my brother. They started searching for in my brother's car, and my father was angry telling my brother to get their badge number, and my brother was giving them attitude, and they finally released them. My brother asked, "why did you frisk us and check us," and the police claimed that they fit the description of a suspect, and my brother responded, "yeah Mexican right," and he got my father and left. It was hilarious because even though at the time it was not funny, my sister and I could just imagine the entire ordeal, and how afterwards they were joking around because they would jokingly say, "Hey did they find the drugs you had hidden in your trousers?" and they would just laugh. Memories and stories like that can keep you in gratitude that they lived and where in your life.

Another time we were in high school, and the Lakers lost to the bulls to win the NBA championship, and when that happened my father was so upset, screaming, and we were laughing. He yelled at us, and said, *"Siempre contra mi, siempre contra mi, usted y usted ya no se pongan mis camisetas."* It was hilarious, he yelled at us, "you are always against me, always against me, you and you need to stop putting my Lakers' shirts on." So, to this day, my siblings and I say those words out loud to each other.

My grandfather had sayings all the time, and we as kids learned those sayings, and we use them when appropriate, and in a way, it keeps the memory of my grandfather alive. He was very wise, and very resilient. I think anybody who survived the *Great Depression* is extremely resilient. I understand now why he would make us eat everything off our plate, and why he would say, "you best eat today because tomorrow we might not have any food." He would say those things because that is how life was like during the *Great Depression*. My grandfather was a saver, and he lived below his means. He always believed in saving for a rainy day, and my grandparents rarely ate out. All the food they ate was cooked at home. My grandfather believed in paying everything in cash, and I remember that his credit cards expired and were not renewed because he did not use them. My grandfather was the disciplinarian, and when we would get in trouble, he would spank the oldest and unfortunately, it was my brother, Tony. My grandfather was a man of authority that no one messed with. Since my mother died, my father would often leave us at my grandmother's house to be taken care of. One day we got in trouble and my grandfather hit me on the head with a shoe, and there was another time he hit my cousin with a bone. It was not funny at the time, but now we think it is hilarious. I find myself saying his sayings, "s*e quebro una taza, cada quien pa' su casa*," "*cada chango pa' su mecate*," and "*el que es buen gallo, donde quiera canta.*" The first saying means, "a mug has shattered. It is time for everyone to go home." In other words, there is a problem in a get together, and it is time for people to go home. This is true in a lot of cases because I have used it when I have lost friendships, or even a relationship that may not have worked out, and I think it is time to go, something has shattered, and it is time to go. The next saying means, "every monkey to his vine," and this one was helpful to me because it meant that everyone had their proper place. Sometimes things happen and they are difficult to understand, but if you think that each monkey has their own place it can make sense that person does not belong with you, and you must go to your own vine and move on. By far the last saying was the message that really impacted me the most. I had a lot of insecurity growing up and even in my adulthood. The last saying means that "a good rooster will perform in any setting." This was meaningful to me because I moved to California, and I was applying for jobs and was deeply insecure about my abilities, but I remembered my grandfather and what he said that if you are a good rooster, you can succeed anywhere. That saying gave me a belief in myself that I needed to take a risk to find a job, and work in teaching at the young age of twenty-two years old. I loved my job, but if it were not for that saying, I am not sure if I would have taken the risk necessary to even try to teach at that age. The sayings of our loved ones keep them alive, but they also put us in gratitude because they left us priceless irreplaceable lessons that we can never forget.

My uncle used to say, "*ya se acabo la escuela y no aprendió.*" Every year when the school year was over, he would ask us what we learned, and we could not say or respond to his question, and he would say that. What that means is "school ended, and you did not learn." To some extent it was true, but we as kids thought that what he said was so funny, we would use it over and over when someone made a mistake. We would say that saying, or when someone would drop something, or spill something we would use that saying. Even as adults we still use that saying because we think that it is hilarious when we make mistakes, and we point out that our sibling went to school and did not learn. Our loved ones love us so very much and when we can laugh at their sayings or memories, we can then shift our attitude and get into gratitude.

One of the things you can do to get gratitude is to thank your emotions. You can say thank you feelings for sending me the message that I am sad, take a moment to feel your feelings, and then release them. You can make a list of all the reasons you are grateful for this person being in your life. How did this person make you feel? Write out a list of intangible things that this person did for you that filled your life. What words of encouragement or affirmations did this person offer you? Then write specifically about acts of service that they did for you. Maybe they took you and picked you up from school. Maybe they cooked for you, sheltered you, and took you to fun places. What gifts did they give you tangible or intangible? Did they buy you something special? Did they make you feel special on your birthday? What about physical affection? How often did they show you their love in an affectionate way? Did they hug you when you needed them to? How about spending time with you? Write about the moments they spent time with you and made you a priority. When would they block out time from their schedule and say this is your time and only your time. These are all the way our loved ones can love us, and in that we can write a list of all the things they did for us and be grateful. If we make this list, and carry it when we are sad, we can shift into gratitude because we were loved by this person, and this list confirms it and reminds us that love is never-ending and it continues on after death.

There was a woman who lost her three daughters in a car accident. When she lost her girls, she was completely devastated, and she went to several mental institutions to try and deal with the hurt and the trauma. This poor woman had to heal and let go of the hurt and bitterness because those emotions separated her from her daughters. She had to focus on the love she had for those girls, and the love they had for their mother because the angry feelings were hurting her instead of helping her. Once she recognized this, she worked really hard to find peace through the tragedy. She recognized that love moved through time and space. The love that she has for her daughters is never-ending, and she holds onto that love because that gives her purpose for living. This woman is a symbol of resilience and overcoming adversity for such a tragic loss, and yet in order for her to feel and be with her daughters she must love and keep giving and receiving love.

She gives her love to others to honor her daughters. The most powerful force in the universe is love, and love keeps us connected and fills all our empty spaces. Love can give us peace and hope, and holding on to the love and gratitude of our loved ones keeps us alive, but it also keeps their essence alive. That is why it is so important to hold on to love because it is forever, and it never dies.

Forgiveness

I know that not all of us have loving relationships with our loved ones. At times, we have estranged relationships with our brothers, sisters, cousins, or parents. Sometimes these people die, and they leave us without closure or unresolved issues. I want to urge you to find forgiveness for these individuals. Not forgiving is an anchor that keeps you trapped in a pit of despair. If you do not forgive, it robs you of the freedom and peace you deserve. You must release the pain. It is even more difficult to forgive someone who has passed because there is no closure or resolution. I cannot tell you why things happen, but I honestly believe no matter what it is, things happen for the greater good and for a higher purpose. I know it is hard to accept and it is not right, but pain and hurt teach you compassion, love, and understanding.

There was a story of a woman who had been married to a man for twenty years, and he told her that he was leaving her. He said he had an affair and had a baby with another woman, and he was leaving right then and there. It just so happened that on that day, he went to the doctor and was told that he had terminal cancer, and he had a short time to live. He told his wife that he was going to go into hospice care at their home. The wife was still angry and said, "you can go with your mistress," and he said, "no, only you know how to take care of me." She talked it over with her brother, and her brother said, "if you are going to take care of him, do it from the kindness and the love of your heart; otherwise, do not do it." He said, "it is your choice, but if you choose to take care of him, do it out of love; otherwise, do not do it." She had to enter the process of forgiveness right away, and in taking care of him, she achieved true forgiveness. When he died, she was sad, but was at peace because she in her moral code did the right thing in taking care of the man who betrayed her, and in the end, he was grateful for her love. It is better to forgive your loved ones while they are alive, but if you cannot, then you must enter into the process of forgiveness in their death.

I am so sorry for the pain and hurt they must have caused you, but it is your responsibility to heal. Even when a person dies, you can still hold resentment in your heart for what they did to you in life. Hoarding pain does not serve you, and the only way to recede the pain is through the process of forgiveness.

Forgiveness is very difficult because we struggle to let go of the pain, and we feel that if we hold on to the resentment against a person it will protect us from getting hurt again. However, forgiveness is often misconstrued. We think it is for the other person, but in reality, it is for ourselves. Forgiveness gives us the freedom to find peace and free ourselves from pain. Forgiveness is a process. At times, we may feel we have forgiven a person, but in reality, true forgiveness happens when you no longer feel pain associated with what happened. If you talk about the injustice done against you, and it still hurts; you may have entered into the forgiveness process, but you have not completely forgiven because you are not totally healed.

Understand that forgiveness is a process, and it takes time to enter into forgiveness. The most important thing is to be gentle with yourself. Love and accept yourself as a human who makes mistakes, and who learns from his/her struggles. Sometimes, you want so badly to forgive, but you have to understand that there are factors to consider when forgiving. For example, you have to contend with your inner self. Your inner child will rebel and make it difficult for you to forgive, and he/she will constantly say it is not fair. This is a normal part of the process. Other times, your anger will sweep in, and your ego will scream he/she does not deserve forgiveness. Sometimes you can fall into a deep depression, and be a victim and ask the unanswerable questions as to why did this happen to you. There is no answer, but all I can say is you can live, learn, and forgive. Forgiving someone does not mean that what they did is acceptable.

Always remember that hurt people hurt others, and most of the time when someone hurts you it really is more about them than it is about you.

Sometimes reliving trauma can be so overwhelming that it makes it difficult to continue. That is okay, listen to your heart, soul, and intuition and continue when you are ready. You might have several people to forgive, so you might have to go through this process continuously, but that is okay. The more you heal, the more you can find peace, and the more you can set yourself free from the pain. The best analogy I can give you is to imagine a prison. Visualize a prison and each cell is a person who has hurt you. As you look around, you see all the people in your lifetime who have hurt you, but all of a sudden you notice that you are in a cell as well, and you are jailed. The only way for you to get out of your cell is to forgive each individual and set them free. When you do, you set yourself free. That is what forgiveness does.

If you are choosing to forgive someone who has passed. I want you to start with a prayer, and I want you to say, "God, I know this person is no longer with us, and I carry all this pain in my heart because of what he/she did to me. I want to thank you for the opportunity to work through my resentments. I am tired of carrying around this load of hurt and pain. Please give me peace and clear me of all the hurt and sorrow from my past. Help me see that everything happened to me to make me stronger, wiser, and to give me the ability to love. Give me the courage and the strength to get through this process. I know you are with me guiding me, and all I want is to have peace through forgiveness and letting go. Thank you for your love, and all the lessons you have taught me. I am forever grateful for you always being there with me. Thank you!" If you have to read this prayer for thirty days until you are ready to forgive this person, then pray this prayer for thirty days. Once you feel ready to forgive you can go into the next process.

This part is difficult because it is probably going to bring up triggers that are going to take you back to being that little child and experiencing that pain. If that happens, I want you to do the following. If you have to step away from the exercise for a bit, then do so, but remember once again feelings are meant to be felt and when they are felt, thanked, accepted, and the message received then they can be released. If you are triggered you can do this, say "I am here now, I am okay, I am safe, that person can no longer hurt me, I am strong, I am loving, and I will protect my inner child." If that does not work, step away, shield your inner child, and tell him/her I got you, you are going to be fine. Now, write a list of all the offenses this person has committed against you. Once you write the list, rank it from least to greatest. Feel every emotion that comes through the memory. Since you have not forgiven, you are going to feel pain. Sit with your emotions for a bit, then tell your emotions, thank you for the message, thank you for being there, and then say, "you can go, thank you."

Now this part can be done in two ways: you can choose the first item on your list, and you can write down what happened, what they did, and how they hurt you. Next, you must allow yourself to feel your feelings and lean into them. Or if you do not want to write down what happened, then you can visualize it, but you must lean into your feelings and feel your emotions and embrace them. Then talk to your inner child and tell him/her you are safe, you are loved, you are okay, I am here. Then write a letter from them to you telling you everything you wished he/she would have said to you. An example is as follows; this is a letter I wrote as if a friend from high school who had passed was writing it to me:

Dear Erica,
I am so sorry for all the hurt I caused you. I made you believe things that were not true. I made promises I could not keep, and I was not a friend that could honor you. I know I hurt you terribly, and I do not deserve your forgiveness. I told lies about you, so other people would not like you. I took away opportunities that you could have had because I was jealous. I tried to be your friend, but I could not be a friend with integrity. I know I did not show you how much I really cared, and I am sorry I hurt you, but knowing that me hurting you was one of my biggest regrets. I am sorry and I hope you can forgive me.
Love,
Your friend

Now visualize this person saying this to you or handing you the letter. Then you say out loud, "I receive your apology…. I receive your sorry…. I forgive you…. say it over and over till you feel peace…I receive your apology… I receive your sorry…. I forgive you …."

You can include all the offenses in one letter, or you could write one letter for each offense, and you repeat the process over and over until you reach the point of truly receiving this person's forgiveness.

At this point, many people say, but he/she is not sorry, and he never said this. Remember what we talked about in the beginning, forgiveness is not about the other person. It is for you, and these exercises are for you to find healing and let go. Whether the person is sorry or not is irrelevant, you have to find forgiveness to set yourself free from the prison of resentment.

Understand that this person may not have been capable of giving you the love you needed or deserved. That means that a person may have been damaged and may not have been capable of having a friendship, or an honest relationship, and their actions showed that. Forgiveness is setting yourself free from pain. Some people do not have the skill set to be honest and have integrity in their relationships. This could have been the case for the person you are trying to forgive.

If doing this exercise is not enough, another thing you can do is write a letter saying everything you wanted to say to them and say it out loud. Speak your pain, your truth, and all the words you wished you would have said, but this must be written down, so it could be your true self. Then read the letter, feel into the feelings, thank your feelings, thank the message, and then release your feelings.

I pray you find forgiveness for those people who hurt you. I pray that you free yourself from the pain, and that you can make peace with the past. I pray you get yourself out of the unforgiveness cell and you let go of whatever hurt and pain no longer serve you. Through prayer you can send this person who hurt you love.

My Father's Eccentricities

My father was full of life
He was passionate about his Lakers
He once threatened us to never wear
His shirts when the Lakers lost to the bulls

He would always say, *siempre contra mi*
That meant we were always against him
He was so angry that we were laughing when his
Lakers lost
Against Michael Jordan

My father was vocal
He was a take it or leave it type man
And he said what was on his mind
He did not trust people

But he was a great judge of character
He would say she is not a good friend
Or he would tell my brother
No te juntes con ese cabron

And he was always right
Our friends would betray us
Or they would get us in trouble
Or they were bad influences

My father was not embarrassed
My sister and I were both in high school
We were on the bottom floor at the mall
All of a sudden from the top floor

There is this man yelling
Almost crazily
"Jessica, Erica"
Disregarding that they were people around
To let us know it was time to go

My sister and I pretended
It was not us
We looked around
And kept walking

Till we nonchalantly went to meet him in the second floor
He was furious
"Why did you not respond when I called"
"Uh…uh our high school friends saw"
"I don't give a shit!!! About your friends"

He would drop us off
In his dilipadated Chevy truck
The door was held closed with a hook
And without fail as we got off,

He would scream
As if on purpose
Dios las bendiga
And we would get embarrassed

He is long gone now
But those moments
Bring me laughter today
It was his way of showing love

His way of saying
Those are my daughters
And with so much adoration
I am their father

The thing we often fail to see
As teenagers
Fathers who scream
Or send a blessing

Are just showing love
No need to be embarrassed
Had we known then
What we know now

We could have stood proud
And said "Yes,
That man screaming
Is my father!"

About the Author

Erica Castro is a Xicana English high school teacher who has taught for twenty five years. She is dedicated to helping and empowering her students. She is a poet that feels that poetry can help people heal their inner-self. She has dedicated herself to publishing student work. She published student art, poems, and story in the Oracle school anthology. She has recently launched Daxson Publishing to publish marginalized voices. She has published Rosalilia Mendoza's *Lili of the Valley*, Adrian Fuerte-Campos *In Solace* coming out in July. She is publishing her poetry book *The Pain Left Behind: Surviving a Suicide Loss*. She is also publishing *Creating Peace through the Grieving Process*, a book that helps you deal with the loss of a loved one. She is also publishing *Mariposa de Fuego: A Journey to Empowerment* by Peruvian born author Áurea María Altamirano Cuaresma coming out in July. She participated in suicide attempt survival collaboration called *Alive to Thrive*. She has also written in two other book collaborations *Badass Within*, and *Healing and Growth: Inspiring Stories for Massive Transformation*. She just released another book collaboration called *Graceful Growth* Series about dealing with loss and grief of suicide.

Connect with Erica: Instagram: ericalopez74

Publishers Note

Daxson publishing was created to help marginalized artists publish their work, so the world can hear their voice. The vision for this publishing house is to help people get their work out there, and not have them struggle finding their way through the publishing process. Everyone's voice deserves to be heard, and we are here to help. If you are interested in submitting a manuscript, email daxsonpublishing@ gmail.com.

www.ingramcontent.com/pod-product-compliance
Lightning Source LLC
Chambersburg PA
CBHW051328120626
46547CB00015B/2448